Manage Stress And Anxiety In Minutes!

FROM CHAOS

TO

CALM

A Comprehensive Guide To Managing Stress And Anxiety In Women

DR. LORRAINE BLALOCK

TABLE OF CONTENTS

INTRODUCTION

In the fast-paced world we live in, stress has become an ever-present companion, and anxiety, its close sibling, often lurks just around the corner. These companions are not exclusive to any one demographic, but their impact on women is distinct, both in its prevalence and manifestation.

The experiences and challenges women face in today's society are unique, and so are their responses to stress and anxiety. The demands of career, family, relationships, and societal expectations can create a complex web of stressors that affect a woman's physical and emotional well-being.

This book is a roadmap, a guiding light to navigate the turbulent waters of stress and anxiety. We will delve into the core aspects of these challenges, exploring the very definition of stress and anxiety, understanding their root causes, and acknowledging the distinct gender perspective that shapes these experiences for women.

We'll take a holistic approach to stress and anxiety, recognizing their physical and emotional toll on the female body. From examining the impact of stress on our physical health to understanding how emotions play a pivotal role, we'll uncover the intricate relationship between mind and body.

But we won't stop at merely understanding the problem. This guide is replete with practical strategies to help women regain control over their lives, from lifestyle changes and mindfulness practices to exercise, diet, and strategies for better sleep. We'll explore resilience and the science of bouncing back from adversity, offering you the tools to develop your inner strength.

Moreover, we believe that a journey towards calmness should not be a solitary one. In these pages, you'll discover the importance of seeking support and therapy and find guidance on how to build a network of care and understanding.

At the heart of this book is the conviction that women can thrive beyond stress and anxiety. We'll explore how to strike a balance in life, set and achieve goals, and ultimately embrace a state of calmness and contentment.

The path to **"FROM CHAOS TO CALM"** may be challenging, but it's a journey worth embarking on. Within these pages, you will find the knowledge, wisdom, and support you need to regain control, overcome obstacles, and emerge stronger than ever. This is your guide, your companion on the road to a calmer, happier you.

CHAPTER ONE

UNDERSTANDING STRESS AND ANXIETY

Once upon a time in a peaceful village nestled between rolling hills and meandering streams, there lived a young woman named Eliza. She was known for her kindness, intelligence, and a warm smile that could brighten even the gloomiest of days. Eliza had dreams as vast as the open sky, and she aspired to achieve greatness in all she pursued.

However, there was a silent storm brewing within her heart, a tempest that she carefully concealed from the world. It was the weight of stress and anxiety that she bore alone, often feeling like a shadow she couldn't escape.

One sunny morning, while strolling through a fragrant meadow, Eliza met an old woman, Agnes, who was known as the village's wise sage. Agnes's eyes sparkled with wisdom, and her presence exuded a sense of tranquility that drew Eliza toward her.

"Dear child," Agnes said, "I sense a burden in your heart. Would you like to share your worries with me?" Eliza hesitated but found herself pouring out her feelings. She spoke of the never-ending expectations she faced as a daughter, sister, and friend. She spoke of the pressure she put on herself to excel in all her endeavors. She spoke of her fear of judgment and failure.

Agnes listened with understanding, her gentle eyes never leaving Eliza's. "My dear," she said, "you are not alone in your feelings. Many women bear the weight of stress and anxiety silently. It's important to understand that these burdens are not a sign of weakness but a reflection of the complex world we live in."

Agnes then shared her wisdom with Eliza. She taught her the importance of self-compassion and self-care, explaining that it was not selfish but essential for her well-being. She encouraged Eliza to seek support from her loved ones, to share her fears and worries, and to let them in.

As the days turned into weeks, Eliza began to apply Agnes's teachings. She opened her heart to her family and friends, finding solace in their understanding and empathy. She started prioritizing self-care, allowing herself moments of relaxation, and discovered the healing power of meditation and mindfulness.

Slowly but steadily, the storm within Eliza's heart began to subside. The once relentless waves of anxiety and stress began to calm. She realized that understanding her own emotions, seeking help, and being kind to herself were the keys to managing her mental health.

As time passed, Eliza not only achieved her dreams but surpassed them. She became an inspiration to others, not just for her accomplishments but for her courage to speak openly about the challenges she faced. She dedicated herself to helping women in her village and beyond, guiding them to understand their own stress and anxiety and supporting them in their journeys to wellness.

And so, the story of Eliza became a testament to the strength that resides in acknowledging and understanding stress and anxiety. Her story illuminated the path for many women to find their own peace and light in the midst of life's challenges.

DEFINING STRESS AND ANXIETY

Stress and *anxiety* are common terms in today's demanding world. While often used interchangeably, they are distinct emotional and psychological states with unique characteristics. This chapter will provide clear definitions of stress and anxiety, offer examples of each, and explore the implications of understanding these states for our mental well-being.

Stress

Stress is a natural and evolutionary response to perceived threats or challenges. It triggers a "fight or flight" reaction in our bodies, preparing us to deal with a difficult situation. Stress can be categorized into two types: acute stress, which is short-term and often beneficial, and chronic stress, which is long-lasting and potentially harmful.

Examples of Stress

Work Deadline: A looming project deadline can cause stress, motivating a person to focus and complete tasks efficiently.

Exams: Students often experience stress before exams, which can push them to study and perform well.

Traffic Jam: Being stuck in a traffic jam on the way to an important meeting can create acute stress, urging individuals to find alternative routes.

Anxiety

Anxiety, on the other hand, is a persistent and excessive worry or fear about future events, situations, or perceived threats. It is a prolonged state of unease that doesn't necessarily relate to an imminent challenge. Anxiety can range from mild to severe and can be categorized into various anxiety disorders, including generalized anxiety disorder, social anxiety disorder, and panic disorder.

Examples of Anxiety

Generalized Anxiety Disorder: Constantly worry about various aspects of life, like health, finances, or relationships, without a specific cause.

Social Anxiety Disorder: Extreme fear of social situations, such as public speaking or attending social gatherings, even when they are not inherently threatening.

Panic Disorder: Sudden and intense episodes of fear, often accompanied by physical symptoms like rapid heart rate, sweating, and shortness of breath.

Understanding the differences between stress and anxiety is crucial for mental well-being. While stress can be a motivating factor, chronic or overwhelming stress can lead to anxiety. Recognizing the transition from stress to anxiety can help individuals seek appropriate support and coping strategies.

Stress and anxiety are distinct but interconnected aspects of the human experience. Stress is a natural response to challenges, while anxiety is a prolonged state of unease. Recognizing the differences and managing both effectively is essential for maintaining good mental health and overall well-being.

Highlights

1. Stress and anxiety are distinct emotional and psychological states with unique characteristics.
2. Stress is a response to perceived threats or challenges, while anxiety involves persistent and excessive worry or fear about future events.
3. Stress can be categorized into acute and chronic stress, with examples such as work deadlines and traffic jams.
4. Anxiety can manifest as generalized anxiety disorder, social anxiety disorder, and panic disorder, with examples including constant worry and fear of social situations.
5. Stress can motivate individuals, but chronic stress can lead to anxiety disorders.
6. Understanding this transition can lead to appropriate support and coping strategies.

CHAPTER TWO

THE GENDER PERSPECTIVE

In the realm of mental health, the gender perspective is an essential lens through which we can explore the intricate experiences of stress and anxiety. While stress and anxiety affect individuals of all genders, there exists a significant gender-based disparity in how these conditions are perceived, experienced, and managed. Here, we delve into the unique gender perspective of stress and anxiety in women, shedding light on the factors that contribute to these disparities and the implications for women's mental health.

I. The Gendered Nature of Stress and Anxiety

Women, across diverse cultures and backgrounds, tend to experience stress and anxiety differently from men. This gendered nature can be attributed to several factors:

Sociocultural Expectations: Societal norms often place higher expectations on women regarding caregiving, nurturing, and emotional labor. These expectations can contribute to stress and anxiety as women juggle multiple roles, such as being mothers, partners, and professionals.

Discrimination and Gender Bias: Women may face gender-based discrimination and bias in various aspects of life, including the workplace, which can lead to chronic stress and anxiety.

Hormonal Factors: Hormonal fluctuations during the menstrual cycle, pregnancy, and menopause can influence emotional well-being and exacerbate anxiety in some women.

Trauma and Gender-Based Violence: Women are disproportionately affected by gender-based violence, including physical and emotional abuse. These experiences can lead to profound stress and anxiety.

II. Disparities in Seeking Help

The gender perspective of stress and anxiety also reveals disparities in seeking help and mental health treatment:

Stigma: Societal stigmas surrounding mental health are often stronger for women, discouraging them from seeking help for fear of being labeled as overly emotional or unstable.

Underdiagnosis: Women's symptoms of stress and anxiety may be underdiagnosed, as they may present differently than men. This can result in delayed or inadequate treatment.

Cultural and Gender Norms: Cultural norms and expectations can dictate that women prioritize the well-being of their families over their own, making them less likely to seek help.

The gender perspective of stress and anxiety in women is vital for creating a more equitable and empathetic approach to mental health. By acknowledging the unique stressors women face and working to reduce disparities in seeking help, we can promote better mental health outcomes for women and a more inclusive approach to mental health for all.

Highlights

1. Women often experience stress and anxiety differently due to sociocultural expectations, discrimination, hormonal factors, and experiences of trauma and gender-based violence.
2. Stigmas related to women's mental health, underdiagnosis of symptoms, and cultural and gender norms can create barriers to seeking help for stress and anxiety.
3. Recognizing these disparities is essential for addressing them.

CHAPTER THREE

CAUSES AND TRIGGERS OF STRESS AND ANXIETY

Stress and anxiety are prevalent mental health issues that affect individuals across all genders. However, women, in particular, face a unique set of causes and triggers that contribute to their heightened vulnerability to these conditions.

I. Sociocultural Expectations and Gender Roles

Sociocultural norms and traditional gender roles continue to place significant pressure on women. These expectations often encompass roles as caregivers, homemakers, and emotional anchors within families. The desire to fulfill these roles while also pursuing a career and personal aspirations can create overwhelming stress.

Example: A woman juggling a full-time job, caregiving responsibilities for children and aging parents, and domestic chores may experience stress due to the societal expectation that she must excel in all these roles.

II. Workplace Challenges

Women frequently encounter unique challenges in the workplace, including unequal pay, limited career opportunities, and gender discrimination. These disparities contribute to professional stress and anxiety.

Example: A woman who faces wage inequality or struggles to advance in her career due to gender bias may experience heightened stress and anxiety related to her professional life.

III. Hormonal Fluctuations

Hormonal changes, such as those during the menstrual cycle, pregnancy, and menopause, can affect women's emotional well-being. Fluctuating hormones can lead to mood swings, anxiety, and even disorders like premenstrual dysphoric disorder (PMDD).

Example: A woman experiencing PMDD may endure intense anxiety, irritability, and depression in the weeks leading up to her menstrual cycle.

IV. Gender-Based Violence and Trauma

Women are disproportionately affected by gender-based violence and sexual assault. Traumatic experiences, whether recent or past, can lead to post-traumatic stress disorder (PTSD) and chronic anxiety.

Example: A survivor of domestic violence may develop anxiety and stress-related disorders due to the ongoing threat of abuse and the psychological scars left by the experience.

V. Caregiving Burden

Women often take on the role of primary caregivers for children, elderly family members, or individuals with special needs. This caregiving burden can be physically and emotionally taxing, contributing to chronic stress.

Example: A woman providing round-the-clock care to a disabled family member may experience stress and anxiety due to the physical and emotional demands of the role.

VI. Stigma and Societal Pressure

Women may face more significant societal pressure when it comes to seeking help for mental health issues. Stigmatization of mental health problems and the fear of being labeled as "emotionally unstable" can deter women from seeking treatment.

Example: A woman with symptoms of anxiety might avoid seeking therapy or medication due to societal expectations that she should be able to manage her emotions without outside help.

VII. Multiple Role Juggling

Women often find themselves balancing multiple roles and responsibilities, such as mother, wife, employee, and caregiver. The constant juggling of these roles can lead to chronic stress.

Example: A woman who is a mother, spouse, and career professional may struggle to meet the demands of each role, leading to stress and anxiety as she strives for perfection in all areas.

Understanding the causes and triggers of stress and anxiety in women is important for both early intervention and support.

Recognizing the unique challenges women face, from sociocultural expectations to workplace disparities, allows for more empathetic and tailored approaches to mental health care. It is essential to empower women to seek help without fear of stigma and to create a supportive environment that acknowledges and addresses the distinct stressors and anxiety triggers they experience.

Highlights

1. Traditional expectations of women as caregivers, homemakers, and emotional anchors can lead to stress and anxiety as they strive to fulfill these roles alongside personal and professional aspirations.

2. Gender disparities in pay, career opportunities, and discrimination in the workplace contribute to professional stress and anxiety for women.

3. Hormonal changes during the menstrual cycle, pregnancy, and menopause can lead to mood swings, anxiety, and conditions like PMDD.

4. Women disproportionately experience gender-based violence and trauma, which can lead to anxiety disorders such as PTSD.

5. Women often bear the burden of caregiving for family members, leading to chronic stress due to the physical and emotional demands of this role.

6. Women may face more significant societal pressure and stigma when seeking help for mental health issues,

potentially deterring them from seeking treatment.

7. The constant balancing of multiple roles, such as mother, spouse, employee, and caregiver, can contribute to stress and anxiety as women strive for perfection in each area.

CHAPTER FOUR

THE PHYSICAL IMPACT OF STRESS ON THE BODY

Stress, an inherent part of human existence, affects individuals of all genders. However, the physical impact of stress often manifests differently in women due to biological and hormonal differences. Understanding how stress takes a toll on the female body is crucial for recognizing the importance of stress management and its implications for women's health.

I. Hormonal Responses

One of the most notable physiological responses to stress is the release of stress hormones, particularly cortisol. In women, the intricate interplay of hormones, including cortisol and estrogen, can influence various aspects of physical health:

Menstrual Irregularities: Chronic stress can disrupt the menstrual cycle, causing irregular periods, missed periods, or increased pain and discomfort during menstruation.

Reproductive Health: Prolonged stress may affect fertility, causing difficulties in conception. Additionally, high stress levels during pregnancy can lead to complications and preterm birth.

II. Immune System Suppression

Stress can weaken the immune system, making women more susceptible to infections and illnesses:

Increased Susceptibility to Infections: Chronic stress can suppress the immune response, making women more prone to infections like colds and flu.

Slower Healing: Stress can impede the body's ability to heal, prolonging recovery from injuries and illnesses.

III. Cardiovascular Impact

Stress has a significant impact on the cardiovascular system, potentially leading to heart-related issues:

Hypertension: Chronic stress can elevate blood pressure, increasing the risk of hypertension and heart disease.

Increased Heart Rate: Acute stress episodes can cause a rapid increase in heart rate, which, if frequent, can contribute to heart problems.

IV. Gastrointestinal Disturbances

The digestive system is sensitive to stress, leading to a range of gastrointestinal issues:

Irritable Bowel Syndrome (IBS): Stress can exacerbate IBS symptoms, leading to abdominal pain, bloating, and irregular bowel movements.

Heartburn and Acid Reflux: Stress can trigger or worsen heartburn and acid reflux, causing discomfort and potentially damaging the esophagus.

V. Weight Fluctuations

Stress can lead to fluctuations in body weight, often affecting women differently than men:

Emotional/Binge Eating: Women may be more prone to emotional eating in response to stress, which can lead to weight gain.

Appetite Changes: Stress can cause appetite changes, leading to overeating or undereating, both of which can affect body weight.

VI. Skin and Hair Issues

The physical effects of stress are visible on the skin and hair:

Acne and Skin Problems: Stress can exacerbate skin conditions like acne and psoriasis, and even contribute to premature aging.

Hair Loss: Chronic stress can lead to hair loss and thinning, which can be distressing for women.

VII. Musculoskeletal Tension

Stress often leads to muscle tension and pain:

Tension Headaches: Stress can cause tension headaches, which can be debilitating and affect a woman's overall well-being.

Muscle Pain: Chronic stress can result in muscle pain, particularly in the neck, shoulders, and back.

VIII. Sleep Disturbances

Stress can disrupt sleep patterns, affecting women's overall health:

Insomnia: Chronic stress can lead to insomnia, making it challenging to obtain restful sleep.

Sleep Disorders: Stress can contribute to sleep disorders such as sleep apnea and restless leg syndrome.

The physical impact of stress on the female body is multifaceted, affecting hormonal balance, the immune system, cardiovascular health, the digestive system, body weight, skin, hair, and overall well-being. Recognizing the physical consequences of stress underscores the importance of effective stress management and support systems to maintain women's health and quality of life.

Highlights

1. Stress affects hormones in women, leading to menstrual irregularities and potential reproductive health issues.
2. Chronic stress weakens the immune system, making women more susceptible to infections and hindering the body's healing process.
3. Stress contributes to heart-related problems such as hypertension and increased heart rate.
4. Stress can lead to issues like IBS, heartburn, and acid reflux.
5. Emotional eating and appetite changes in response to stress can lead to weight gain or loss.
6. Stress affects the skin, potentially causing acne and skin problems, as well as hair loss.
7. Stress leads to muscle tension and pain, often resulting in tension headaches and muscle aches.
8. Stress disrupts sleep patterns, causing insomnia and sleep disorders, affecting overall well-being.

9. Recognizing these physical effects underscores the importance of effective stress management and self-care for women's health.

CHAPTER FIVE

THE MIND-BODY CONNECTION

The intricate relationship between the mind and body plays a pivotal role in managing stress and anxiety, particularly in women. While these conditions have psychological roots, their physical manifestations and effects are undeniable. This chapter explores the vital concept of the mind-body connection in stress and anxiety management, focusing on how understanding and harnessing this connection can be a powerful tool for women's mental health.

I. Stress and Anxiety: The Interplay of Mind and Body

Stress and anxiety originate in the mind, often in response to life's demands, challenges, and uncertainties. However, the physical symptoms they trigger are significant:

Psychological Symptoms: Stress and anxiety manifest as excessive worry, fear, restlessness, and difficulty concentrating. These thoughts and emotions significantly impact the mind.

Physical Symptoms: Stress and anxiety are often accompanied by a range of physical symptoms, including rapid heart rate, muscle tension, headaches, and gastrointestinal distress. These symptoms directly affect the body.

II. The Mind-Body Connection

The mind-body connection is a bi-directional relationship, where emotional and mental states influence physical health, and vice versa. In stress and anxiety management, the interplay between these two domains is evident:

Physiological Response to Stress: When the mind perceives a threat or challenge, it activates the body's "fight or flight" response, releasing stress hormones such as cortisol. This physical response primes the body to respond to the stressor.

Physical Tension: Anxiety, especially, is associated with muscle tension and physical discomfort. These bodily sensations can feed back into the mind, intensifying feelings of worry and fear.

III. Harnessing the Mind-Body Connection for Stress and Anxiety Management

Recognizing the mind-body connection offers valuable tools for managing stress and anxiety:

Mindfulness and Relaxation Techniques: Practices like mindfulness meditation, deep breathing exercises, and progressive muscle relaxation can calm the mind and alleviate physical tension. By relaxing the body, women can reduce anxiety and stress levels.

Physical Activity: Regular exercise not only improves physical health but also promotes mental well-being. It reduces stress hormones and stimulates the release of endorphins, which enhance mood.

Diet and Nutrition: Nutrient-rich diets can positively impact mental health. Avoiding excessive caffeine, sugar, and alcohol can help stabilize mood and reduce anxiety.

Counseling and Therapy: Cognitive-behavioral therapy (CBT) and other therapeutic approaches address both the mental and physical aspects of stress and anxiety. Therapists teach coping strategies that help individuals manage emotional responses and reduce physiological symptoms.

Medication: In some cases, medications may be prescribed to manage severe anxiety and stress. These medications can target brain chemistry and alleviate symptoms.

IV. Self-Care and Holistic Approaches

Understanding the mind-body connection underscores the significance of self-care and holistic approaches for stress and anxiety management:

Balancing Rest and Activity: Prioritizing sleep and incorporating periods of relaxation in a busy lifestyle can enhance overall well-being.

Healthy Lifestyle Choices: Women can make conscious choices about their diet, exercise, and mental wellness practices to support a harmonious mind-body relationship.

Seeking Support: Women should not hesitate to seek emotional support from friends, family, and healthcare providers. Sharing feelings and concerns can alleviate both mental and physical symptoms of stress and anxiety.

The mind-body connection is an essential consideration in stress and anxiety management for women. Recognizing how emotional and psychological states influence physical health and vice versa provides valuable tools for managing these conditions. By harnessing this connection, women can take a holistic and proactive approach to their mental well-being, fostering resilience and reducing the impact of stress and anxiety on both their minds and bodies.

Highlights

1. Stress and anxiety have both psychological and physical components, with emotional symptoms impacting the mind and physical symptoms affecting the body.

2. The relationship between mental and physical health is bi-directional, with emotional states influencing physical health and vice versa.

3. Women can manage stress and anxiety by utilizing mindfulness and relaxation techniques, engaging in regular physical activity, maintaining a balanced diet, seeking counseling or therapy, and considering medication when necessary.

4. Balancing rest and activity, making healthy lifestyle choices, and seeking emotional support are vital components of managing stress and anxiety through the mind-body connection.

5. Understanding this connection empowers women to take a holistic and proactive approach to their mental well-being.

CHAPTER SIX

HORMONES AND STRESS

The female body undergoes intricate hormonal fluctuations throughout life, making women more susceptible to the physical and emotional effects of stress. Here, we explore the relationship between hormones and stress in women, shedding light on the complexities of this interaction and its impact on mental and physical well-being.

I. The Hormonal Roller Coaster: Women's Hormonal Phases

Women's lives are characterized by distinct hormonal phases, each with its unique set of stress-related challenges. Stress triggers the release of various hormones, with cortisol being the primary player. In women, the hormonal response to stress can be influenced by the menstrual cycle and other life phases:

Menstrual Cycle: The menstrual cycle, with its fluctuations in estrogen and progesterone, is a monthly hormonal journey. The premenstrual phase is notorious for emotional volatility and heightened stress sensitivity. Hormonal fluctuations during the menstrual cycle can affect the stress response. Women may experience increased stress sensitivity, mood changes, and physical symptoms during specific cycle phases.

Pregnancy and Postpartum: Pregnancy introduces significant hormonal changes, often leading to mood swings and stress. The postpartum period, characterized by hormonal fluctuations and sleep deprivation, can increase vulnerability to stress. The stress response during pregnancy can be heightened due to hormonal changes and concerns about maternal and fetal health.

Perimenopause and Menopause: The transition to menopause is marked by fluctuating hormones and hot flashes, both of which can contribute to stress and anxiety. The changing hormonal landscape during perimenopause and menopause can lead to increased stress susceptibility, potentially exacerbating symptoms such as hot flashes and mood swings.

II. Coping Mechanisms and Resilience

While hormonal fluctuations can increase vulnerability to stress, women possess unique coping mechanisms and resilience:

Social Support: Women often place a strong emphasis on social connections, seeking support from friends and family during stressful times.

Hormonal Resilience: Many women adapt to hormonal fluctuations over time, developing a sense of resilience and an understanding of their emotional responses.

Mind-Body Practices: Practices like mindfulness, meditation, and yoga can help women manage stress by regulating the body's hormonal responses.

IV. The Implications for Mental and Physical Health

The intricate relationship between hormones and stress has profound implications for women's mental and physical health:

Mental Health: Hormonal fluctuations can influence mood, contributing to conditions like premenstrual syndrome (PMS), postpartum depression, and perimenopausal mood disturbances.

Physical Health: Chronic stress can lead to physical health issues, including cardiovascular problems, weight fluctuations, and sleep disturbances, all of which can be influenced by hormonal factors.

Reproductive Health: High stress levels can impact fertility and menstrual regularity, affecting reproductive health.

The interplay between hormones and stress in women is a complex and often underestimated aspect of their lives. Hormonal fluctuations across different phases can impact the stress response and emotional well-being. Understanding this relationship is crucial for women to develop effective coping strategies and support systems that enhance their mental and physical health. It also highlights the importance of a holistic approach to women's well-being, taking into account both psychological and hormonal factors in stress management and overall health.

Highlights

1. Women go through distinct hormonal phases in their lives, such as the menstrual cycle, pregnancy, postpartum, perimenopause, and menopause, each of which can affect their stress response.

2. Stress triggers the release of hormones, with cortisol being a primary player. Hormonal fluctuations in women can influence their stress response and exacerbate stress-related symptoms during specific life phases.

3. Women often use social support, hormonal resilience, and mind-body practices to manage stress effectively.

4. The relationship between hormones and stress has significant implications for women's mental health, physical health, and reproductive health.

5. Understanding this connection is crucial for developing effective coping strategies and holistic approaches to well-being.

CHAPTER SEVEN

ANXIETY AND IT'S MANIFESTATIONS

Anxiety is a pervasive mental health issue that affects individuals of all genders. However, women often experience anxiety in distinct ways due to a combination of biological, sociocultural, and psychological factors. Understanding anxiety's manifestations in women is crucial for early recognition, effective support, and improved mental health outcomes.

I. The Gendered Nature of Anxiety

The relationship between gender and anxiety is a complex and nuanced topic, but it's an important one to explore. Research suggests that women may be more prone to anxiety than men, and this may be due to a number of factors. Some of these factors include sociocultural expectations around gender roles, the experience of stress, and biological factors. Let's explore these factors further. Women's experiences with anxiety are influenced by a variety of gender-specific factors, including:

Biological Factors: One biological factor that can contribute to anxiety in women is the hormone estrogen. Estrogen is thought to play a role in the brain's response to stress, and some research has suggested that high levels of estrogen may be linked to increased anxiety. Additionally, hormonal changes during certain times in a woman's life, such as during pregnancy or menopause, can also impact anxiety levels. Hormonal changes during the menstrual cycle, pregnancy, and menopause can influence anxiety levels. For example, premenstrual syndrome (PMS) can lead to mood swings and anxiety.

Another biological factor that can contribute to anxiety in women is through the fight-or-flight response. When faced with a stressful situation, the body releases hormones like cortisol and adrenaline, which can lead to physical and psychological symptoms of anxiety. The fight-or-flight response is a normal biological reaction that's meant to help us respond to danger or threats. However, when this response is activated too frequently or for too long, it can actually cause anxiety. This can be especially true for women, who may be more likely to experience chronic stress. When stress becomes chronic, it can affect the brain's ability to regulate anxiety levels.

Sociocultural Expectations: Societal norms often place higher expectations on women to fulfill roles as caregivers, nurturers, and emotional anchors. These expectations can contribute to anxiety as women navigate multiple responsibilities. One sociocultural expectation that can contribute to anxiety in women is the pressure to be perfect. There is often an unrealistic expectation that women should be able to "have it all" - a successful career, a happy family, and a perfect appearance. This can lead to anxiety about not being able to meet these expectations.

Another example of a sociocultural expectation that can contribute to anxiety in women is the pressure to be slender in size. Women are often bombarded with images of idealized, unrealistic body types in the media, and this can lead to body image concerns and anxiety. Additionally, there is a double standard that women should be both thin and attractive, while men are not held to the same standards. Another socio-cultural expectation that can contribute to anxiety in women is the pressure to be a "good mother." Mothers are often expected to prioritize their children over their own needs, and this can create anxiety around balancing the demands of motherhood with other aspects of life. Additionally, mothers are often judged harshly if they don't meet these expectations, which can create even more anxiety.

II. Emotional Manifestations of Anxiety

Anxiety in women often manifests through a range of emotional responses:

Excessive Worry: Women with anxiety tend to ruminate and worry excessively about a wide range of concerns, including family, work, and personal matters. One emotional manifestation of anxiety in women is excessive worry. This is when a woman may feel anxious or worried about a situation, even when there's no real danger. She may spend a lot of time thinking about possible negative outcomes, or feeling like she's always on edge. Some common worries for women include concerns about relationships, work, finances, and health. Let's look at some examples of how this might look in real life.

One example of excessive worry might be a woman who is constantly worrying about her relationships. She may overthink conversations with friends or family members, worrying that she's said or done the wrong thing. She may also have trouble relaxing or enjoying time with others, because she's always thinking about what could go wrong. Another example might be a woman who is always worrying about money, even when her finances are in good shape. She may constantly check her bank account and avoid spending money, even on necessary items.

Social Anxiety: Another common emotional manifestation of anxiety in women is social anxiety. This is when a woman feels nervous or uncomfortable in social situations. She may feel like everyone is judging her, or that she's not good enough. As a result, she may avoid social situations altogether, or only participate in them with a lot of anxiety and stress. Social anxiety can make it difficult to make friends, network, or enjoy social activities.

Social anxiety in women is when a woman feels especially anxious in social situations, to the point where it interferes with her life. This anxiety can be triggered by things like meeting new people, going to parties, or even just answering the phone. The woman may worry that she will say or do something embarrassing, or that others will judge her. She may also avoid social situations altogether, or have physical symptoms like a racing heart or sweating when she's in social situations. It's important to note that social anxiety isn't just shyness - it's a much more intense form of anxiety.

Emotional Sensitivity/Irritability: Women with anxiety may exhibit heightened emotional sensitivity, experiencing intense reactions to stressors and perceived threats. Irritability is another common emotional manifestation of anxiety in women. This is when a woman feels more easily frustrated or angered, even by small things. She may find herself snapping at people, or having difficulty controlling her emotions. This irritability may be related to stress or anxiety, and can make it difficult to maintain relationships or deal with everyday situations. One example of this might be a woman who feels irritable at work, finding it difficult to get along with colleagues. She may snap at her coworkers or find it difficult to focus on her work.

Anxiety can lead to irritability, making it challenging for women to manage their emotional responses, particularly in stressful situations. When it comes to irritability, there are a few specific things that may be happening. One is that the woman's stress response may be heightened, meaning that she reacts to even small stressors with a "fight or flight" response. This can lead to irritability and anger. Another factor may be that the woman is experiencing chronic fatigue due to the stress. This can cause her to be more irritable and less able to tolerate frustration.

III. Physical Manifestations of Anxiety

There are several physical manifestations of anxiety, and they can vary from person to person. Some common physical symptoms include muscle tension, headaches, stomach upset, sleep problems, and trouble concentrating. Other possible physical symptoms include heart palpitations, increased heart rate, sweating, dizziness, and shortness of breath. Many people also experience changes in appetite or digestive problems. Physical symptoms like these are the body's way of responding to stress.

For women specifically, there are some additional physical symptoms that may be experienced. For example, some women experience hot flashes, while others experience issues with menstruation. Hot flashes are when a woman suddenly feels warm and may start sweating, with redness in her face and neck. These flashes can be very brief or last several minutes. They may happen at any time, even in the middle of the night. Anxiety can cause irregular periods, or periods that are heavier or lighter than usual. There may also be changes in libido or sexual desire. It's important to note that the physical symptoms of anxiety in women can be related to other health issues, so it's important to speak with a doctor about any new or unusual symptoms. Anxiety in women can also manifest with these physical symptoms:

Muscle Tension: Many women with anxiety experience muscle tension, particularly in the neck, shoulders, and back, which can lead to pain and discomfort.

Gastrointestinal Distress: Anxiety can trigger symptoms like nausea, diarrhea, or stomachaches, often impacting women's digestive health.

Sleep Disturbances: Anxiety can cause difficulties falling asleep and staying asleep, leading to sleep disturbances that exacerbate emotional and physical symptoms.

IV. Cognitive Manifestations of Anxiety

Anxiety often affects cognitive processes in women in ways which includes:

Rumination: "Rumination" is a term used in psychology to describe a pattern of repetitive and negative thinking. Rumination is when a person keeps thinking about something over and over again, even if it's negative or unhelpful. It can involve replaying events over and over in your head, or going over "what if" scenarios. It's often accompanied by negative feelings like anger, regret, guilt, and frustration. This type of thinking can be unhelpful and can make anxiety worse.

One common cognitive manifestation of anxiety in women is rumination. It can be like being stuck in a loop of negative thoughts. Women may engage in rumination, dwelling on distressing thoughts or situations, which can intensify anxiety symptoms.

Negative Self-Talk: Anxiety can lead to negative self-talk, where women criticize themselves or doubt their abilities, contributing to a sense of self-doubt and insecurity. Another example is catastrophizing, which is when a person thinks of the worst possible outcome in a situation. These cognitive manifestations can be very distressing and difficult to manage.

V. Coping Mechanisms and Support

There are a number of coping mechanisms and sources of support that can be helpful for women experiencing anxiety. One example is **cognitive behavioral therapy (CBT)**. CBT is a type of therapy that helps people recognize and change unhelpful thinking patterns and behaviors. It can be a very effective treatment for anxiety.

Another example is **mindfulness meditation**, which is a practice that involves focusing on the present moment and accepting your thoughts and feelings without judgment. Another coping mechanism is **engaging in creative pursuits**. This could be anything from painting or drawing to writing or playing a musical instrument. Creative activities can be a great way to express yourself and help you relax and de-stress.

Finding a community of like-minded women is another source of coping mechanisms. This can be online or in-person. Many women find that connecting with others who are going through similar experiences can be very helpful. There are also many support groups for women with anxiety, which can provide a safe space to share experiences and receive support.

Exercise also helps in releasing endorphins, which are chemicals in the body that improve mood and reduce stress. It can also increase overall feelings of well-being. Some examples of physical activity that can be beneficial for anxiety include yoga, running, and walking.

VI. Implications for Mental Health

There are definitely some implications for mental health when it comes to anxiety in women. One implication is that anxiety can lead to other mental health conditions, like depression or substance abuse. It's also associated with physical health conditions like high blood pressure, heart disease, and digestive problems. In addition, anxiety can have a negative impact on relationships, work, and daily functioning. Anxiety symptoms can interfere with daily life, affecting work, relationships, and overall well-being. Women may be at an increased risk of developing anxiety disorders, including generalized anxiety disorder, panic disorder, and social anxiety disorder.

There's another implication that's really important to be aware of, and that's the stigma around mental health conditions. Women with anxiety may face negative stereotypes or discrimination, which can make them less likely to seek help. Stigma can also make people feel ashamed or embarrassed about their condition.

VII. Encouraging Open Dialogue and Seeking Help

Breaking down the stigma around anxiety and mental health conditions in general is crucial. One way to do this is through open dialogue. By talking about anxiety and other mental health conditions in an open and honest way, we can help to normalize them and reduce the stigma. Promoting open dialogue about anxiety and encouraging women to seek help is vital for addressing anxiety's manifestations:

Reducing Stigma: Reducing the stigma associated with mental health issues is essential to make women feel comfortable seeking treatment.

Early Intervention: Early intervention and treatment can help women manage anxiety and prevent it from becoming chronic or leading to other mental health conditions.

Anxiety manifests uniquely in women due to a combination of biological, sociocultural, and psychological factors. Recognizing the gender-specific manifestations of anxiety is a critical step in improving mental health outcomes. By promoting open dialogue, reducing stigma, and encouraging women to seek help, we can provide effective support and foster better mental well-being for women facing anxiety.

Highlights

1. Women's experiences with anxiety are influenced by hormonal fluctuations and societal expectations.
2. Anxiety in women often leads to excessive worry, irritability, and heightened emotional sensitivity.
3. Women with anxiety may experience muscle tension, gastrointestinal distress, and sleep disturbance.
4. Anxiety can result in rumination and negative self-talk, affecting cognitive processes.
5. Women use coping strategies such as social support and mind-body techniques to manage anxiety.
6. Women may be at increased risk of anxiety disorders, impacting their daily functioning and overall well-being.
7. Reducing stigma and promoting early intervention are essential for addressing anxiety in women and improving mental health outcomes.

CHAPTER EIGHT

THRIVING BEYOND STRESS AND ANXIETY

Thriving beyond stress and anxiety involves not just managing these feelings but also harnessing them as catalysts for personal growth, resilience, and a more fulfilling life. This chapter explores the concept of thriving beyond stress and anxiety, offering insights into the strategies and practices that can empower individuals to turn adversity into opportunity.

I. Recognizing Stress and Anxiety

Stress and anxiety often manifest in various emotional, cognitive, and physical ways. These responses are part of the body's natural defense mechanisms, preparing individuals to respond to perceived threats. However, chronic stress and anxiety can have detrimental effects on mental and physical health, making it essential to recognize their presence.

II. Shifting Perspectives

Thriving beyond stress and anxiety begins with a shift in perspective. Rather than viewing these emotions solely as obstacles, individuals can reframe them as signals for growth and transformation. This new perspective acknowledges that adversity can be a powerful catalyst for positive change.

III. Building Resilience

Resilience is the ability to bounce back from adversity and adapt positively to life's challenges. It involves strengthening emotional, psychological, and physical resilience factors to better withstand stress and anxiety. It is the ability to recover from difficult experiences and come out stronger. It's not about being immune to stress, but rather about finding ways to adapt and cope with it. In the face of adversity, resilience can help us to find meaning and purpose, and to grow as individuals.

IV. Coping Strategies

As mentioned earlier, effective coping strategies empower individuals to manage stress and anxiety.

Practicing mindfulness and meditation can help individuals stay present and reduce rumination, a common feature of anxiety. These techniques promote emotional regulation and resilience. Maintaining a healthy lifestyle through regular exercise, a balanced diet, and adequate sleep is essential for managing stress. Physical well-being provides a solid foundation for resilience.

Building a support network of friends, family, and professionals offers emotional safety nets during difficult times. Sharing concerns and seeking guidance can enhance resilience. Developing emotional intelligence enables individuals to recognize, understand, and manage their emotions effectively. It empowers them to navigate stressors more skillfully.

Cognitive-behavioral techniques, such as reframing negative thoughts, challenge cognitive distortions and empower individuals to adapt more resilient responses to stress and anxiety. Also, therapeutic approaches, including cognitive-behavioral therapy (CBT), provide valuable tools for managing anxiety and stress and addressing their underlying causes.

V. The Growth Mindset

A growth mindset is a way of thinking that's focused on learning, growth, and progress. It's the idea that we can always improve and develop new skills, even in the face of challenges. When it comes to stress and anxiety, a growth mindset can be a powerful tool. By focusing on learning and growth, rather than on perfection or avoiding failure, women can find new ways to thrive and cope with stress. A growth mindset is the belief that challenges are opportunities for growth and learning. This perspective helps women reframe stressors, viewing them as catalysts for personal development and increased resilience.

VI. Thriving Through Adversity

Thriving beyond stress and anxiety involves using these emotions as fuel for personal growth and self-improvement. It means recognizing that adversity can provide valuable lessons and serve as a stepping stone to greater resilience and happiness.

Another way to thrive is to practice gratitude. Gratitude is the practice of focusing on the things we're thankful for, even when things are tough. It can help us to shift our focus away from negative thoughts and feelings, and towards the good things in our lives. Research has even shown that gratitude can have a positive impact on our mental and physical health.

VII. Self-Compassion

Self-compassion is crucial for thriving beyond stress and anxiety. It involves treating oneself with kindness, understanding, and empathy, acknowledging that setbacks and challenges are part of the human experience. Focus more on self-care. Self-care is about taking care of our physical and emotional needs, and it's especially important when we're dealing with stress and anxiety. Self-care can take many forms, like exercise, eating healthy food, getting enough sleep, and spending time with loved ones.

VIII. Resilience in Action

The transformation from managing stress and anxiety to thriving beyond them involves taking concrete steps to integrate resilience into one's life. These steps can vary from person to person but often include:

- Setting achievable goals and maintaining a sense of purpose.
- Cultivating positive relationships and engaging in social activities.
- Embracing a growth mindset and viewing challenges as opportunities for growth.
- Practicing self-compassion and self-care.
- Continually seeking self-improvement and personal development.

Thriving beyond stress and anxiety is not about eliminating these emotions but rather transforming them into opportunities for growth and personal development. By shifting perspectives, building resilience, employing effective coping strategies, and embracing a growth mindset, individuals can navigate life's challenges with greater strength, purpose, and fulfillment. Ultimately, thriving beyond stress and anxiety is about recognizing that resilience

is not only possible but also a powerful path to
a more fulfilling life.

Highlights

1. Embrace stress and anxiety as catalysts for personal growth and transformation rather than as obstacles.
2. Strengthen emotional, psychological, and physical resilience to better withstand and recover from stress and anxiety.
3. Utilize mindfulness, physical well-being, social support, emotional intelligence, cognitive restructuring, and professional help to manage stress and anxiety effectively.
4. Embrace challenges as opportunities for personal development and growth.
5. Treat oneself with kindness and empathy, acknowledging that setbacks and challenges are part of the human experience.
6. Take practical steps to integrate resilience into daily life, including setting achievable goals, maintaining positive relationships, and practicing self-care.

CHAPTER NINE

EMBRACING CALM

She was known for her tranquil demeanor, always greeting life's challenges with a serene smile and had a secret to her calmness, a secret born out of her personal battle with anxiety and stress. Her name is Maya.

Maya's journey with anxiety began during her early years. She was a sensitive soul, deeply affected by the world's worries and her own self-doubts. As she grew older, her anxiety became a constant companion, coloring her interactions and decisions.

One day, Maya decided that she had had enough. She yearned for a life free from the heavy burden of anxiety. She began her quest for serenity with small, mindful steps. She started by connecting with nature, walking barefoot on the earth, and listening to the rustling leaves. These simple acts grounded her and reminded her of the beauty in the world.

Maya also delved into the world of meditation and yoga. She discovered that these practices not only calmed her racing thoughts but also offered profound insights into her own mind. Through mindfulness, she began to observe her anxious thoughts without judgment, like clouds drifting through the sky.

But Maya's journey was not just about individual healing; it extended to the community she cherished. She initiated a women's support group in the village, where they would gather under the shade of an ancient tree to share their experiences, fears, and hopes. These gatherings provided a space for women to find solace in each other's stories and embrace the warmth of companionship.

One evening, as the sun cast a warm glow over the hills, the women of the village gathered for one of their meetings. They sat in a circle, sharing their tales of triumph and struggle, laughter and tears. Maya, who had become a beacon of calm, spoke to them about embracing stress and anxiety as catalysts for growth.

She explained that anxiety was not an enemy but a messenger, a signal that something needed attention or change. It was a natural response to life's uncertainties. With her wisdom, she encouraged the women to see anxiety as a teacher, guiding them to a deeper understanding of themselves.

Over time, Maya's approach resonated with the women of the village. They began to view anxiety as a path to self-discovery, a tool for transformation. The serene stream that passed through their village was a symbol of their journey – constantly flowing, embracing obstacles, and finding a way forward.

Maya's legacy of calmness and her perspective on anxiety became a guiding light for the village women. They learned to find solace in nature, practice mindfulness, and gather in their circle of support. Together, they embraced the flow of life, with its ups and downs, understanding that serenity could coexist with stress and anxiety.

The village continued to thrive, and the women, inspired by Maya's wisdom, found a deeper connection with their inner selves and with each other. Anxiety was no longer a source of fear but a companion on their journey to self-discovery, a reminder that embracing life's uncertainties could lead to a richer, more fulfilling existence.

You too can live and learn from Maya and strive to become a better version of yourself. The story above is more of an illustration to becoming a resilient woman amidst life's struggles. I'm rooting for you all!